NATURE

A Collection of Poems

Torie Cooper

Blue Wattle Press

Cover Illustration: Torie Cooper
Derived work based upon Bob Jagendorf's photograph,
"A Tiger in the Water"©

Copyright © 2017 Torie Cooper
All rights reserved
ISBN: 0999085603
ISBN-13: 978-0999085608

For Nana

Acknowledgements

I would like to thank my family and friends in both Australia and the United States for their encouragement and support. In particular, I am greatly indebted to the wise and wonderful poets at Changing Hands Bookstore's Poetry roundtable in Tempe, Arizona. Without your guidance, friendly critiques, and gentle nudging, I might never have published this book. Special thanks go to my niece Kate Holaren for editing portions of the typescript. Also, I would like to thank the Jagendorf family for kindly allowing me to place my tiger painting upon the cover of this book. My painting is based upon a photograph by the late Bob Jagendorf who was a talented photographer and I hope it would have pleased him to see his wonderful tiger making the rounds in another form. I would also like to thank Charles Portolano, editor of *The Avocet* for promoting the importance of reading and writing nature poetry. Finally, I would like to pay homage to Saint Francis of Assisi – poet, nature lover, and advocate for peace.

Table of Contents

Acknowledgements	v
Broken Shells	13
Wanderer	14
The Walker	15
Elephant Memories	17
The Grazer	19
Saguaro Waits	20
Raven in the Mist	21
Ice-Bear	22
First Outing	24
Dandelions in the Field	25
Bushfire	26
Curiosity	27
The Fight	28
Sand Crawler	30
Love in the Everglades	31
The Runners	32
Watching Dawn	34

Wombat Walk	35
Startled	36
Birthing Mountain	37
Old Cockatoo	39
The Carnivore	40
Pause	41
Rough Start	43
Storm Conductor	45
Guardian	46
Hidden	47
Protector	49
Koala on Fire	50
Gone	52
Garden Feast	54
Silent Ambush	55
Downhill	56
Breaking Sky	57
Wings of the Sea	58
Bush Summer	59

Tree-top Grooming	60
Drought	62
Midday Moment	63
Winter Trail	64
Ball Roller	66
Mesquite Drops	67
Sea Voyage	68
Devil's Feast	70
Life in Motion	71
The Last Thylacine	73
Encounter	74
Full Circle	76
Fire Cat	77
Forgetful Beach	78
Afterward	79
List of Flora & Fauna	80
Notes	82
About the Author	83

In a world older and more complete than ours they move finished and complete, gifted with extensions of the senses we have lost or never attained, living by voices we shall never hear. They are not brethren, they are not underlings; they are other nations, caught with ourselves in the net of life and time, fellow prisoners of the splendor and travail of the earth.

Henry Beston, *The Outermost House*

Broken Shells

The irritable surf
spits out
remnants of seashells
upon cold, moist,
compact sand.
Broken,
calcified homes
abandoned by their owners.

Smashed against
limpet infested,
slippery and jagged rocks
of ancient continents,
agitated waves
randomly
wash and toss
shell fragments
across tide pools and sand.

Mingling with
salty driftwood,
pebbles and odorous
rotting seaweed,
shattered shells
form a diverse carpet
for the exploring webbed feet
of gulls and plovers.[1]

Wanderer

High above corrugated sea,
she glides freely,
without effort.
Pale,
salmon-colored beak,
long rigid wings
slicing through layers
of cool, crisp, salty air,
strong wind ruffling
gray-brown feathers.

Laysan albatross,
a thousand miles
from grass,
sand, and stone
wanders,
drifting through endless
blue-gray landscape,
far from the small
Hawaiian island
of her hatching.

Lifted high
upon invisible air currents,
albatross closes
her soft dark eyes;
living, breathing, resting
within a vast
supportive world
of sky and sea.

The Walker

Dank fur smelling of
cold river water,
hangs limp and thick
about his body,
remnants
of shredded pink salmon
still wound among
long gray-black claws.

Brown bear slowly walks,
slightly pigeon-toed
over smooth,
rounded stones,
damp driftwood;
large thick pads
splaying beneath his feet.

Quiet for all his weight,
brown bear
moves methodically
along the flat curved bank,
past clumps
of lupine's final display
of purple-blue flowers.

Enormous wet brown nose
sniffing, flaring,
twitching upon bear's
massively broad face;
a living thing unto itself,
gathering information.

Small amber eyes
focused just ahead of him
reflect soft purple glow

of day's end,
smeared
like fading watercolor
across mountain-framed horizon.

Darkening dense forest
of Sitka spruce,
Western hemlock, Red alder,
huddle nearby,
branches touching,
cradling restful birds.
Brown bear walks
in lingering light,
belly full.

Elephant Memories

Warm fluid streams
from the facial glands
of young adult elephant
as she gently fondles
the smooth
sun-bleached bones
of her mother.
Soft, prehensile tip
of long muscular trunk
tenderly tracing
the familiar shape.

An awkward,
long-legged calf,
wobbly and restless
stands by her side,
born too late
to know of and learn
from his remarkable
grandmother.

Quietly,
the remaining herd
approaches,
bodies and trunks
swaying in ancient rhythm.
Columnar legs
ending in wide
thickly padded feet
compress
the tired aching earth,
stirring up thin cloud
of reddish-tan dust
as they walk.

Sunset's gentle amber glow,
softly bathes
gray wrinkled skin,
highlighting dried mud
embedded
within deep grooves;
transforming
the herd's collective skin
into a living map
of past journeys.

Hard, parched ground
where the old matriarch fell
has become a sad
yet sacred place;
the loud reverberating thud
of her collapse
long since faded.
Small herd stands together
in silent unified reverence,
caressing the bones
of their beloved
. . . remembering.

The Grazer

Manatee's squared mandibles
plough through
lush green seagrass
like a Saturday morning
lawnmower.
Fleshy, prehensile lips
sprouting stiff whiskers
feel, curl, grasp
tender stalks
as flexible pectoral fins
gently scrape
sandy, silty bottom
stirring up clouds of debris.

Flattened, fan-like tail
propels large rotund body
through warm river water,
as miniscule eyes
scan aquatic horizon.

Manatee's broad curved back,
scar-riddled,
reflects encounters with
ribbed boat hulls, propellers;
flesh-chiseled stories of life
shared alongside humans.
Manatee's ceaseless
search for sustenance,
precarious.

Saguaro Waits

Thirsty for sky water
Saguaro shrinks,
ribs almost touching,
withdrawing into itself
amidst the harshness
of Sonoran desert summer.
Long needle-like spines
crisscross pale green skin
forming sharp botanical armor;
hungry animals
dare not risk a single bite.

Searing sun silently
scrapes, scorches
a long, painful trail
across wide cloudless sky.
Saguaro's upheld arms
tirelessly beg the heavens
for cool, cleansing water.

Shallow, shriveled roots
patiently wait in the dark
for months on end,
awaiting life sustaining
moisture to penetrate
hardened, desiccated soil.
Arid desert life:
a delicate balance
for survival.

Raven in the Mist

Sage-gray morning,
raven flaps
large iridescent wings
through misty forest rain.
Thick black beak
parting heavy moist air
like the nose of an airplane.

Cool clear drops of water
spill across his face,
guard hairs keep nostrils dry.
Nictitating membranes
and black-lashed eyelids
cover and uncover the eyes
like opposable
windshield wipers.

Beads of water
roll across his powerful
chest and back,
tumbling off stiff tail feathers;
gravity-pulled droplets
free falling,
splattering upon cold,
damp woodland floor
pelting crisp, dried leaves
and broken gray twigs,
softly drumming an ancient song.

Raven flies onward
to a destination
known only to him;
a cause that cannot wait
for rain to grow weary.[3]

Ice-Bear

No trees, no structures
impede powerful, frigid winds
slamming ice-bear's back
as she sits upon
blue-tinged, salty sea ice.
Gusts parting
thick transparent fur,
black skin absorbing
warmth
from drowsy sunlight.

Ice-bear turns her head
at faint sound,
pointing enormous black nose
toward pale azure sky,
analyzing subtle messages
carried aloft.

Sensing nothing of interest,
massive hind legs slowly
push down against thick ice,
lifting her colossal weight.
She stands and shakes.
Loose dense fur,
muscles, and blubber
ripple,
while long sharp claws
puncture the ice
anchoring her in place.

Ice-bear ponderously walks,
large thickly furred paws
plodding toward
a familiar place
where ice

meets choppy, dark blue sea.

Long rays fired
from falling arctic sun
softly pierce
liquid brown eyes.
Ice-bear blinks
into stiff wind
as she scans the far horizon
of her frozen world.[2]

First Outing

Wolf pups leave
familiar earthy smell
of warm dark den,
following slender, lanky mother
as she jaunts
into brilliant daylight;
tiny blue eyes squinting.

First breeze blows
ticklish through soft,
mottled fur
as first shadow
follows bounding
pint-sized bodies,
awkward, stubby legs.

First whiff of Spring lupine
clings to inquisitive
black noses,
while spongy soil,
wild grasses, stones, twigs,
meet cushiony
untouched paws.

Eyes track butterflies,
swaying bushes;
observe fallen logs,
tall thick stands of Douglas fir,
other excited pack members.

Mother wolf watches pups'
first moments of discovery
beyond safety of comfortable den;
now, life lessons begin.

Dandelions in the Field

A playful breeze
meanders
through clusters
of small yellow petals.
Dandelions grow
in wide grassy field
gazing upward
as wispy high clouds
race one another
across cerulean sky
with no finish line.

Beneath cool,
dark earth,
slender hairy roots
grasp the soil
with curled, clenched fingers;
parts never seen or touched,
anchors for growing
green bodies above.

Delicate,
swaying dandelions
release precious
fluffy seeds
upon the wind,
tumbling, twirling,
flying across the field;
botanical gymnasts
performing
in the Olympics of life.

Bushfire

Dingo's large moist nose
detected fire
long before thick,
particulate smoke
stung deep brown eyes.

Cacophony of
crackling, roaring,
exploding eucalyptus trees
assault his sensitive
hearing.

Swirling orange embers
swarm like bees,
twist like tornados,
fly like bullets
in powerful wild winds.

Dingo cannot avoid
hot rain of fire
singeing his coarse tan fur.
Heavily padded paws
dance painfully
upon hot mixture
of blackened soil,
smoldering ash.

His heightened senses
make instantaneous
adjustments,
countering
bushfire's moves;
a dangerous game of chess.

Curiosity

Humpback whale calf
holds his enormous,
dill pickle head
above water.
Large glistening eye
peering inquisitively
at noisy
fishing boats,
whale watching vessels.

Calf's massive mother
floats nearby,
she is the color
of battleships,
protectively placing herself
between her precious calf
and the objects
of his curiosity.

The Fight

Savage,
unbridled power,
terrifies savannah creatures
into running, hiding.

Two male African lions
fight over females,
territory;
testosterone fueled combat
brutal, deadly.

Wide, scarred muzzles
contract into frightening
wrinkled snarls,
stiff whiskers horizontal,
curled lips revealing
enormous canines:
enameled
stalactites, stalagmites
within a cavernous mouth.

Rearing up upon
powerful hind legs,
muscles rippling,
lions ferociously battle,
lost within
churning, choking cloud
of dirt, flying fur.

Massive paws
equipped with curved,
razor-sharp claws
angrily lash out,
deeply slashing flesh.
Teeth sink into thick

protective manes,
ripping out mouthfuls
of tawny-colored hair.

Cries of pain mingle
with thunderous,
reverberating roars,
short fur drenched
in a violent mixture
of blood and dust.
'King of the Jungle'
fights for his kingdom,
his life.

Sand Crawler

Scorpion crawls
upon tiny feet
across shifting
North African sand,
pincers held wide
ready to embrace
the doomed.
Crystals of sand
once sparkling
in searing summer sun
now shimmer
in cool night air
beneath
a voluminous moon.
Scorpion is hungry
and the night is long.
Unsuspecting prey
do not see him
or hear him coming.
Soon,
he will be satisfied.

Love in the Everglades

Intense, vivid moonlight
falls upon warm,
murky swamp.
Thousands of buzzing insects
join large chorus
of droning bullfrogs,
chattering Black-crowned
night herons.

Twenty American alligators
float together,
eagerly awaiting
Spring's tryst.

Rows of prehistoric
osteoderms line
tops of dark gray heads,
broad backs,
and long powerful tails;
barely breaking swamp's
calm, glowing surface.

Bulbous,
golden-colored eyes
sparkle like living jewels,
retinas reflecting celestial light.

Congregating en masse,
alligators follow
ancient instinctual urge;
preparing to mate
in balmy,
bug-infested swamp.

The Runners

Small herd of female giraffe
run between scattered
acacia trees across wide
amber-green savannah
nostrils flaring,
avoiding purposeful,
prowling lions.

Tall thick necks
supporting heavy heads,
rock back and forth
like a child's rocking horse,
in rhythm with
long galloping legs,
knobby knees.
Multiple hefty hooves
pound the earth,
kicking up
choking clouds
of dirt, grass, debris.

Tufts of soft dark hair
atop rounded horns
and stiffly bristled
brown manes,
blow in
self-created breeze.
Thin whip-like tails
spin wildly in circles
beneath
gently sloping backs.
Giraffes' bodies;
a living, moving canvas
of russet-colored patches.

Reaching a safer location,
giraffe herd gradually
slows then halts,
catching
their collective breath.
Good visibility,
plentiful green leaves,
twigs, and fruit;
ensure safety for all
to rest, to browse.

Watching Dawn

Australian raven sits alone,
ample onyx beak
facing warm rising sun,
dark feet curled comfortably
upon eucalyptus's smooth
gnarled branch.
Easy summer breeze
tenderly ruffles
black-satin feathers,
reflecting soft iridescence.

Wooden gum nuts
bursting with
tiny vermillion flowers
and slender
sage-green leaves,
drum lightly upon
mottled gray boughs
playing a delicate,
hushed tune.

Raven's attentive
pearl-white eyes,
framed by deep black lashes,
survey a timeless landscape
generations of raven
have gazed upon.

Sun continues rising,
pouring greater light
over far horizon
of the Australian bush.
Silently, raven rests
simply being.

Wombat Walk

Wombat's rotund
brown body waddles along
well-worn bush trail
lined with dry grasses,
looking like
a wine barrel with legs.
Pudgy padded feet
move softly, quietly
upon shifting,
waterless soil.

She pauses,
large dusty nose
pressed to the ground,
nostrils twitching,
wallaby
has crossed her path,
his long heavy tail
leaving scented drag marks;
the smell familiar,
non-threatening.

Further meanderings
bring other discoveries:
marsupial mice burrows,
clawed footprints
of lumbering goanna,
magpie droppings.

Wombat ignores them,
toddling onward,
hunger driving her journey;
the smell of approaching
rain heavy in the air.

Startled

Harbor seal's discovery
results in unexpected
face full of black ink;
expanding dark cloud,
confusing.

Giant Pacific octopus
rapidly shoots
from sandy sea floor
like a blazing rocket,
eight salmon-colored tentacles
trailing behind large,
bulbous head.

Quickly finding refuge,
octopus slides head first
into dark rocky crevice,
hastily reeling long
suction-cupped tentacles
behind herself;
stuffing her flexible body
into the irregular-shaped space.

Octopus quietly waits,
protective cloud of ink
gradually disperses;
harbor seal searches
for easier food elsewhere.

Birthing Mountain

Fuji can't breathe
deep beneath the earth;
soil clogged, crushed,
boiling under pressure.
Fuji must release,
move, expand.

Trembling
earthquake contractions
give way to
explosive cries.
Fuji is birthed
into the biosphere
like a baby thrust through
its mother's birth canal.

Pushed,
propelled upwards,
smashing through
earth's protective shell
of bedrock,
past the shallow
kingdom of worms,
Fuji blasts
into a new world.
Toxic gas, ashen clouds
expelled
with each fiery,
sputtering breath.

Scratched, scraped,
wounded,
thick bloody lava
flows down crevices
of Fuji's exhausted body.

Slowly,
contractions cease.
Fuji rests,
wounds healing
with time
into quiet dormancy.

Old Cockatoo

Icy cold day,
Sulphur-crested cockatoo
rests atop weathered fence,
gnarled gray feet tucked tight
beneath frail body.
Feeble rays of falling
afternoon sunlight
barely warming
his thin frame.

Tattered
cream-gray feathers,
no longer the radiant white
of his youth,
hang about him.
Expressive,
yellow crest absent
from his aged head.
Bitterly biting air
feeds mercilessly
upon featherless patches
of exposed flesh.

Through a wafer-thin
draughty window,
I watch the ancient bird
close his tired eyes
to sundown's fading light,
my human heart
longing to warm him.

Pulling a woolen sweater
tighter across my chest,
I sip tea,
watching.

The Carnivore

Winged insect thrashes
violently,
trapped in liquid
collected
at bottom of slippery
narrow tube,
unable to free itself.
He will drown,
gradually digested
by hungry Pitcher plant.

Beautiful, bewitching,
pitcher plant's beguiling
red entrance into
waxy elongated body,
deceptively attracts
unsuspecting insects
into her trap;
a 'welcome mat'
inviting guests to enter,
with no exit for the living.

Thriving within
nutrient poor, acidic soil,
pitcher plant
masterfully engages
in treacherous
botanical carnivory;
gaining nourishment
from the unwary,
the dead.

Pause

Thick, moist nostrils
suddenly flare and snort.
White rhino
throws her enormous head
up from the tall
clump of thirsty grass
as though
trying to pierce
the cloudless sky
with her bulky horns;
small bright eyes
unable to see
that which had made
the sudden sound.

She is upwind
of the sable antelope
whose sharp-edged hoof
snapped the fallen, hollow
acacia branch,
dry and brittle as it lay upon
the desiccated savannah soil.

Rhino pauses,
assessing.
Cup-like ears
fringed with tiny sensitive hairs
rotate like giant satellite disks
scanning the air.

When all appears safe,
she relaxes and blinks,
eyelashes golden
in late afternoon light.
Massive muscles,

again lowering
her gargantuan head
down to the pale
green grass
that sustains her.

Rough Start

Green turtle hatchling,
buried deep,
breaks free
from gooey egg shell;
swimming vertically
through mottled darkness,
soft heavy sand,
straining to breach
crumbling surface
of a new world.

Dawn's gentle light,
moderate breezes,
caress tiny
olive-green body,
shield-shaped carapace.
Wind-blown grains
of speckled sand
adhere to large,
moist eyes.

Frantically clawing along
ancient ancestral path
toward clear,
frolicking waters,
hatchling answers
Coral Sea's inner call.
Small,
flexible flippers
row rapidly to and fro
across wide beach;
a minuscule
reptilian rowboat.

Squawking,
marauding seabirds
form predatory gauntlet.
Hatchling
struggles relentlessly
towards warm waves
of indifference,
concealing
sharp corals, hungry fishes;
journey for survival
exhausting,
perilous.

Storm Conductor

Currawong sits defiantly
atop weathered telephone pole,
years of white bird droppings,
faded and fresh
coat grainy,
splintered wood.

Menacing,
runaway thunderclouds
stampede angrily across
heavy, darkening sky.
Flocks of rainbow lorikeets
noisily flee;
currawong remains.

Gray feet firmly grasp
tall man-made perch.
Alone
upon his podium,
currawong
conducts an orchestra
of mayhem:
thunder, lightning,
rain, hail.

Wild, frenzied winds
violently lift currawong's
black and white feathers;
yellow eyes
blink protectively
against flying debris.
Currawong fears nothing,
turning broad black back
against the storm.

Guardian

Gymea lily
stands sentinel,
rigidly rooted upon
small sandstone hill
surveying ferries, yachts,
catamarans
powering through
shimmering waters
of Sydney Harbour.

Thick pole-like stalk,
brilliant green,
peeling yet firm;
pushes through the soil,
reaching ever upward,
aspiring to touch
the midday sun.

Blazing red flowers
explode from
cupped cradling hands
of gigantic unfurled bud.
Unkempt,
elongated bracts
dance wildly;
botanical tongues of fire
licking
wispy white clouds
migrating overhead.[5]

Hidden

Emerald tree boa slithers along
sturdy olive-gray tree limb,
air heavy,
humid.
She is silent,
stealthy, camouflaged,
rainforest inhabitants
do not notice her.

Stretched to full length,
hundreds of tiny muscles
propel her stunning
emerald green body
along damp branch;
no need for hands, feet.

Reaching flat junction
of forked tree,
she effortlessly loops
her long body
into a circular blob
like a living garden hose,
protectively tucking
her graceful head
inside soft center
of her own smooth coils.

Boa rests,
despite open
jewel-green eyes,
long forked tongue
withdrawn inside
sharply toothed mouth;
snake perpetually alert
to vibrations

from predator or prey.

Quiet, motionless,
emerald tree boa
exudes reptilian poise
and beauty
as she basks
in filtered light.

Protector

Silverback crashes
through thick,
lush green foliage
like a runaway
black locomotive;
unstoppable, dangerous.

Long, silvery-black fur
standing stiffly on end,
increases perceived size
of already massive
shoulders, arms, legs.
Powerful pectoral muscles
ripple beneath bare skin
of broad chest;
colossal canines
threateningly flash white
within open
roaring mouth.

Angry,
Mountain gorilla's
enormous hairy fists
clench sizable plant stalks
ripped from their roots;
a trail of trampled,
broken brush
left behind him.

Thundering
into small clearing,
silverback prepares
to lay down his life
in protection of his family.

Koala on Fire

Roaring inferno engulfs the Bush,
wildfire gone mad.
Crazed wind swirls,
mini tornados
spew embers, hot ash
onto parched vegetation
beneath smoky, scorched sky.

Small heart pounding with fear,
koala bounds up nearest gum tree,
clawed hands, feet
providing momentary traction
upon smooth, slippery trunk.
Scrambling as high
as his weight will allow,
koala clings vice-like
to wildly swaying eucalypt.

Thick particulate,
blue-gray smoke
encircles woolen body
with strong smell
of burnt charcoal.
Tiny amber eyes sting painfully;
copious tears spill over
small eyelids,
flowing down the sides of
large black nose.
Blinking doesn't help,
koala tightly closes his eyes,
whining.

No other creature can hear his pain
over forceful, fickle wind
roaring through dry bush,

blowing fire across the canopy
like a frenzied, troubled artist
painting trees with red-orange flame.

Koala's nostrils, throat, lungs,
aspirate ubiquitous smoke.
Surrounding him,
flammable eucalyptus leaves
explode into fiery beasts
licking the coughing,
choking sky,
obliterating the sun.

It won't be long now,
koala's gum tree is becoming
hot against his body.
Soon he will melt to the trunk;
his blackened body
discovered with many others
only after fire and wind
have nothing left to burn.

Gone

Plant fossils rest
within the palm of my hand.
Small gray impressions
in stone
of lives once lived
beneath the very same
stars, moon, and sun
moving overhead this day.

Primordial plants grew
against all possible odds,
reaching upwards
with tendriled fingers
towards the
warmth and brilliance
of a younger sun;
plants competed
with other plants,
other beings.

On cloud darkened days,
cool water,
pure and life-giving
fell from heavy skies
with the fullness
of their own weight,
cleansing waxy plant skin,
drenching rich soil.

At times,
an ancient warm wind
waltzed with these plants,
flexible green bodies
swaying one way
then another,

until their dance cards
were full.

Breast-fed
from Mother Earth,
surviving the appetites of
animals no longer with us,
botanical beings left behind
photographic negatives
within shale;
postcards from the past.

Garden Feast

Blue-tongued skink's
powerful,
conical teeth
grasp and crush
large unsuspecting
garden snail,
shell shattering like glass,
fluid spilling over
rim of skink's lower jaw.
Crunching, swallowing,
he rapidly devours
his moist meal.

Seeking shelter beside
squalid, splintered fence,
reptile flicks wide,
diamond-shaped
blue tongue
into balmy air;
tasting, smelling, sensing.

All safe, he rests;
short, stubby legs
pressed alongside
stout body
like a bather upon a beach,
smooth slick scales
glistening in warm
afternoon light.[4]

Silent Ambush

Agouti's moist nose
senses something above
yet eyes see nothing.
He does not recognize
the dark shape
whose massive body
has blocked
the shimmering stars
strewn across the
southern night sky.

Agouti's hesitation is fatal.
Jaguar silently springs,
with stunning speed
from contorted tree limb
left swaying
beneath his released weight.
Outstretched forearms,
led by scalpel-sharp claws
extend toward the small,
unsuspecting
target below.

Agouti dies upon impact.
Strength and weight snap his spine,
curved claws pierce and tear,
stout canine teeth puncture,
powerful jaws crush.

There is no savagery
on this warm,
clear night in the jungle.
No malice,
only hunger.

Downhill

Milky green glacier water
falls face-first
into cold rushing river
from an unseen source
above barren tree line.

Following path
of least resistance,
pebbles, rocks, debris,
tumble over themselves
in winding race
to the sea.
Stones are smoothed, rounded;
washed by icy-water, silt,
minuscule specks of gold.

Towering Sitka spruce,
swaying in shivering wind
cheer everyone on
from rugged sidelines;
green feathered boughs
full of squirrels and cones.

Bald eagle hungrily follows
river's drunken path
searching for unwary fish
resting among eddies;
chicks wait in the nest.

Runaway river
scours the landscape
deeper, wider;
writing a changing story
in liquid.

Breaking Sky

Midnight,
thunder rolls across
the Illawarra
like a bowling ball
rumbling along
slick wooden floor
forever crashing into pins.

Hungry,
devouring silence,
storm spits out
auditory fury,
tumultuous tremors.

Pugnacious clouds
shoot liquid spears
into bushes, trees, rivers;
washing away soil,
drowning crumbling
parched sandstone.

Bush creatures,
wide-eyed,
hearts pounding
retreat to safety.
Wild sky thrashes
until exhausted.

Wings of the Sea

Majestic Manta ray
slowly flies through
clear tropical waters,
gracefully flapping
enormous pectoral fins
like a giant underwater bird.

Millions
of miniscule plankton
funnel inside manta's
curved cephalic lobes,
entering her
wide-open mouth;
manta ray filters
fast-food on the go.

Black and white body,
wide, gargantuan,
effortlessly traverses
outer edge of coral reef
dwarfing other fishes;
short thin tail
trailing behind
like ribbon in the wind.

Manta's dark shadow
passes over speckled
sandy sea floor
filled with hidden life,
momentarily
blocking the sun
with her elegant form.

Bush Summer

Blazing bugger of a day,
blowflies, mozzies,
seek out shade,
moisture.

Cockatoos gather
among welcoming arms
of elderly fig tree,
softly chortling
to themselves,
eyes closed.

Magpies are quiet,
outside
occasional outbursts
of irrepressible melody.

Cicadas buzz in unison,
a zealous
high-pitched choir,
threatening to drive
every other creature mad.

Leaves hang limp,
no wind
in their sage-gray sails
resting in the doldrums.
Just another
blistering summer day.

Tree-top Grooming

Early afternoon,
upper canopy
hot, humid, quiet.
Scarlet macaw preens
bold, brilliant feathers
against vast backdrop
of South American
rainforest.

Tiny clouds of white powder,
avian dander,
billow briefly in the air,
particles
landing like dandruff
upon macaw's
silky smooth shoulders,
gracefully sloping back.

Large, powerful,
cream-colored beak
skillfully applies oil
to each colorful feather:
scarlet, yellow, green, blue.
Scrupulous care
keeping feathers waterproof,
flightworthy, clean.

Macaw's gnarled gray feet
hold him steadfast
upon slightly swaying
branch;
body contorting
like a yogi as he grooms.

Periodically,
he pauses preening,
listening
for noteworthy sounds.
Keen,
lemonade-colored eyes
scan tree-top canopy,
cloud-speckled sky
for danger.

Relaxed yet alert
atop his high forested perch,
macaw continues grooming;
a meticulous necessity
of daily bird life

Drought

Searing sun scrapes
the parched dome
of a thirsty sky
as it slowly journeys
to Hades' far horizon,
plummeting
over fiery edge.

A sudden, loud *'crack'*
rips open the brittle fabric
of the desiccated heavens,
rain-free thunder intruding
like an unwanted guest.

Sky screams
and thrashes
into purple-black
of early evening,
unable to get comfortable.

Below,
scorched, cracked land
feebly opens its dry mouth
in a futile attempt
to catch
one single, solitary drop
of precious, cool water.

Midday Moment

Noisy miner skillfully wipes
brilliant yellow beak
upon eucalyptus's
slouchy branch,
as if finished
with a messy meal.

Delicate white blossoms
burst thickly from tiny
wooden gum nuts
like vases
overfilled with flowers.
Slender,
sage-green leaves
hang limply overhead,
softly brushing
noisy miner's
gray and yellow feathers.

He is sleepy,
small eyes framed
with tiny lashes,
close briefly in slumber.
Miner caressed by
a mellow midday breeze
meandering through
the old gum.

Winter Trail

Bison herd follow
one another ant-like
through soft deep snow,
leader breaking trail.
Powerful chests,
strong stocky legs,
methodically
plough forward,
swallowed by a surging
ocean of white.

Windblown tsunami
of snowflakes
twist and twirl,
covering vast prairie,
isolated trees,
frozen ponds.

Wide, horned heads
hang low,
leaning into stinging,
untamed wind.
Blankets of fleecy snow
snugly drape
burly broad backs,
humped shoulders;
thick wooly fur
impervious
to moisture, cold.

Warm steamy breaths
escape capacious nostrils,
panting open mouths;
rising,
lingering momentarily

within crisp biting air
like clouds of smoke
in a cigar room.

Bison herd marches forward
searching endless terrain
for hidden food
beneath the snow.

Ball Roller

Small yet mighty,
an Egyptian god,
female dung beetle
rolls treasured ball
of camel poop
across warm, undulating
Saharan sand.

For her,
tiny tan-colored ball
of dried grass remnants
is boulder-sized,
requiring enormous
effort to move.
But dung beetle is
stout, powerful
like a high-performance
compact car.

Tenacious
despite hardship and obstacles,
she rolls dung backwards
using sharply rasped
hind legs;
thin layer of dust
hiding her dull black body.

Arriving
at choice location,
dung beetle
lays her precious eggs
upon her prize;
a ready-made meal
for future hungry offspring.

Mesquite Drops

Tiny elliptical leaves fall
like gentle green rain
from tired old mesquite tree,
lightly blanketing
hard desert soil.
Hundreds fall sideways
with each puff
of warm, whispering wind.

Burnished brown bark,
rough and rugged
partially peels
from tortured trunk
as new growth
expands beneath;
creating inconspicuous places
for sleeping lizards,
secretive spiders.

A pair of delicate Inca doves
walk along
the straighter boughs
heads bobbing,
quietly cooing an ancient
desert song.
Breeze blown leaves
dropping
from branches above,
lightly land
upon their feathered
gray backs;
doves scarcely noticing
mesquite's
soft green shower.

Sea Voyage

Coconut palm leans low,
arcing across narrow
white beach,
prevailing Trade Winds
permanently bending
scarred and pitted
gray trunk.

Palm is heavily laden
with precious seeds,
one of them falling,
splashing into
clear turquoise sea.

Seed is protected
inside brown fibrous shell;
water supply,
dazzling white food
included within.

Coconut shell floats,
bobbing, rolling
atop warm amiable waves,
joining green sea turtles,
paddling gulls, crested terns.
Carried by a gentle,
determined current
from one island
to another.

Washed, stranded
upon solid land,
drying shell cracks open.
Seed sprouts sturdy
green leaf sunward as

slender root tendrils
descend into darkness,
grasping sandy sediment.

Coconut seedling
anchors itself in place,
grand sea voyage over.

Devil's Feast

Banshee screams
erupt into cacophony
of hellish,
other-worldly sounds
breaking stillness, silence
of cool, damp eucalypt forest.
Periodic drumming
of remnant rainwater
dripping upon leaves,
leaf-litter, small stream,
now replaced with high-pitched
shrieks, screeches,
intermittent growls.

Three Tasmanian devils
fight, feed upon
wet wallaby carcass
strewn beneath
partly cloudy night sky.
Powerful,
blood-drenched jaws
crush bone, tear muscle,
shred organs.
Short black muzzles
defensively bite
fellow devil's faces
in frenzied desire
to satiate ravenous cravings.

No sharing equality,
only survival
amidst ghoulish sounds
of demons feasting within
dark, dank,
dripping forest.

Life in Motion

Living sea studded
with midday sunlight,
displays her silver jewels
twinkling atop mild
wind-blown swells.

Within cloudless
azure sky,
opportunistic pelicans dive,
folding broad
brown wings against
streamlined bodies.
Long thick beaks
piercing
dark blue water;
hungry avian intruders
disrupting swirling mass
of panicked,
silver fishes below.

Nearby, flying fishes
frightened
by hunting sharks,
explode from the sea,
fanning long
wing-like fins
upon cool surface air,
gliding like paper airplanes
before jealous gravity
pulls them back
beneath
sun-warmed waters.

Endless wind,
ceaseless current,

life above and below
perpetual motion of the sea,
exchange elements;
stirring the sparkling
aquatic cauldron of life.

The Last Thylacine

He died in the Spring,
the last of his kind.
His final exhale
gentle as the evening breeze
tenderly stroking his old fur.
He didn't see the sun rise
above the distant tree line
that morning,
didn't feel its warmth
upon his still form
lying upon the cool,
hard concrete floor
of his cage.
But somewhere deep
within those staring,
unseeing brown eyes
remained his last dream.
A dream of running free
beside his mate
across field and bush,
of drinking cold, clear water
from a mountain stream,
of feasting upon fresh wallaby
following a long hard chase;
the dream of a thylacine
soul set free.

Encounter

My bloodied hand
called the shark.
She was hungry,
expecting to find
an injured fish
thrashing through
the final throbbing
moments of life.
Instead,
she discovered me.

Curious,
slowly circling
my awkward floating frame,
I became the sun
within
her watery solar system,
the center of
her vast aquatic world.

My eyes followed
her graceful orbit.
Sleek, stunning,
alert to all things.
Dull black
unblinking eyes,
wide sensitive snout
scan my suitability
for further enquiry.

Moments later,
losing interest
shark slowly swam away.
Soft, filtered light
from a sleepy

afternoon sun
warmly bathing
the rough scales
of her asphalt-colored back.
Powerful,
gracefully swishing tail
gradually disappearing
into the swirling
sandy mist
of shallow water,
swallowed by a blue-green
liquid cosmos.

Full Circle

Elderly moose falls hard,
five wolves upon his back.
His final moments
spent in shock
. . . then acceptance
at that which cannot be changed.

Moose has faced danger before
but now,
his old bones won't run.
Large, heavy head rests upon
the moist grass of his birth;
it smells as it always has
of food, survival, life.

Eyes that have witnessed
cycles of twenty summers
and twenty winters,
now become still
and unseeing.
Yet within their stillness
is reflected
the soft glow
of a celestial blanket
thrown across
the clear night sky.
Old moose lies
cradled within
the eternal arms
of heaven and earth.

Fire Cat

Dusk, northern India,
Bengal tiger's thick fur
ablaze
with falling sunlight,
shades of orange, red, amber,
bursting between
deep black stripes.

Tiger walks carefree
through thick stands
of tall grass;
mottled mixture
of faded yellows and greens
parting in his wake
like waves before
the bow of an ocean liner.

Massive,
thickly padded paws
splay silently upon
dry soil, leaf litter.
Salmon-pink nose,
long, stiff white whiskers,
lead the way towards
stream's muddy edge.

Drinking birds take flight
at big cat's appearance.
Alert, yellow eyes glow
like molten gold,
reflecting days'
final fiery rays
as tiger bends low,
raspy tongue lapping
cool refreshing water.

Forgetful Beach

Herring gull glides lazily above
the last of this day's footprints,
remnants of moments gone.
Joy and laughter
imprinted upon
the short-term memory
of loose, shifting sand.
Vanishing footprints,
wind swept and washed clean.
Restless surf and sea,
unsentimental
puppets of the moon,
hold nothing unto themselves.
Forever creating freshness,
erasing the words of life
as they are written.

Afterward

It's my hope you enjoyed reading this small book of nature poetry as much as I enjoyed writing it. If you feel inspired to learn more about the plants and animals featured in these poems then I'll be doubly pleased. You may also wish to write your own nature poems.
Our planet and its unique flora, fauna, rivers, mountains, air and oceans all require our thoughtful care and stewardship. Learning about our world through reading, discussion, and better yet, direct experience and exploration can arm us with useful knowledge and ideas with which we can make a positive difference. Public libraries, Zoos & Aquariums, National Parks, State and Federal Wildlife agencies, and Conservation organizations await our eager and unabashed curiosity and support. With that said, let's go forth, live mindfully upon this earth, and read and write poetry.

List of Flora & Fauna

<u>Birds</u>
Australian Raven (*Watching Dawn*)
Currawong (*Storm Conductor*)
Inca Dove (*Mesquite Drops*)
Laysan Albatross (*Wanderer*)
Noisy Miner (*Midday Moment*)
Pelican (*Life in Motion*)
Raven (*Raven in the Mist*)
Scarlet Macaw (*Tree-top Grooming*)
Sulphur-crested Cockatoo (*Old Cockatoo*)

<u>Fishes</u>
Flying Fish (*Life in Motion*)
Manta Ray (*Wings of the Sea*)
Shark (*Encounter*)

<u>Invertebrates</u>
Dung Beetle (*Ball Roller*)
Giant Pacific Octopus (*Startled*)
Scorpion (*Sand Crawler*)

<u>Mammals</u>
African Elephant (*Elephant Memories*)
African Lion (*The Fight*)
Agouti/Jaguar (*Silent Ambush*)
American bison (*Winter Trail*)
Bengal Tiger (*Fire Cat*)
Brown Bear (*The Walker*)
Dingo (*Bushfire*)
Florida Manatee (*The Grazer*)
Giraffe (*The Runners*)
Gray Wolf (*First Outing*)
Harbor Seal (*Startled*)
Humpback Whale (*Curiosity*)
Koala (*Koala on Fire*)

Moose (*Full Circle*)
Mountain Gorilla (*Protector*)
Polar Bear (*Ice-Bear*)
Rhinoceros (*Pause*)
Tasmanian Devil (*Devil's Feast*)
Thylacine (*The Last Thylacine*)
Wombat (*Wombat Walk*)

Plants
Coconut Palm (*Sea Voyage*)
Dandelion (*Dandelions in the Field*)
Fossils (*Postcards from the Past*)
Gymea Lily (*Guardian*)
Mesquite (*Mesquite Drops*)
Pitcher Plant (*The Carnivore*)
Saguaro (*Saguaro Waits*)

Reptiles
American Alligator (*Love in the Everglades*)
Blue-tongued Skink (*Garden Feast*)
Emerald Tree Boa (*Hidden*)
Green Turtle (*Rough Start*)

Notes

1. Broken Shells – Originally published in *The Avocet*, Summer-2013. Pg. 51
2. Ice-Bear – Originally published in *The Avocet*, Winter-2017. Pg. 52
3. Raven in the Mist – Originally published in *The Avocet*, Fall-2014. Pg. 59
4. Garden Feast – Originally published in *The Avocet*, Summer-2015. Pg. 13
5. Guardian – Originally published in *The Avocet*, Spring-2016. Pg. 30

About the Author

Torie Cooper has always loved wildlife and natural scenery, having grown up in a small community outside Australia's Royal National Park. She studied zoology at Arizona State University and wildlife management at Macquarie University, Sydney. She enjoys spending time with family, friends, and her dog Scotty.

www.ingramcontent.com/pod-product-compliance
Lightning Source LLC
Chambersburg PA
CBHW032209040426
42449CB00005B/512